PARTY OF
One

Also by Sheila Kamuda

My Badass Journal
My Badass Gratitude Journal
The Little Book of Badass Feelings

PARTY OF
One

A memoir about getting through loss,
discovering that you are stronger
than you want to be, and
being okay as a "party of one."

Sheila Kamuda

R
Regan Press

PARTY OF
One

Copyright © 2023 by Sheila Kamuda
All rights reserved. No part of this publication may be reproduced in any form without written permission from the publisher.

For permissions contact
liveoutloudinspire@gmail.com

Cover: Photograph of author from personal collection

ISBN: 979-8-218-31592-4

R
Regan Press

Dedication

To Sydney, whose strength, courage, and inner light helped me heal more than I thought possible.

Contents

Prologue – xiii

Part One – Honor Yourself

Time Is Irrelevant – 4

Being Alone – 6

Wishing You Could Have Done More – 8

Allow Friends to Gather – 10

When Friends Return to Their Lives – 12

Getting Through the Day – 14

Never the Same Again – 16

Wading Through the Bills – 18

Fear Keeps Me Here – 20

Special Days – 22

Holding Hands – 24

The Creative One – 26

Travel Bound – 28

A Paradox – 30

Driving Around – 32

That Voice – 34

Part Two – Believe in Yourself

Stronger Than You Want to Be – 38

What's for Dinner? – 40

A Source of Comfort – 42

Favorites – 44

Bobisms – 46

Baseball – 48

A New Dining Ritual – 50

Tears – 52

No Concentration – 54

Sunday Mornings – 56

Just Lucky I Guess – 58

Part Three — Be Yourself

It's Okay to Do Nothing – 62

Party of One – 64

Going to the Movies. Alone – 66

Feeling Bad Because You're Feeling Good – 68

Getting Back to Who You Are – 70

Keeping Memories – 72

Pardon My French – 74

No More Us – 76

The Chagall Windows – 78

The Movie in My Mind – 80

Part Four — Find Yourself

Sophisticated and Scrappy – 84

So Many Books – 86

Make Your Home Yours - 88

Deep in His Heart - 90

Letting Go of Stuff - 92

Scattered Papers - 94

Paris on My Own - 96

Dear Bob: Letters of Our Life - 98

Celebrate a Life - 100

Maybe It's Me - 102

The Big Move - 104

Epilogue - 106

Loss Is Loud - 110

Acknowledgements - 112

About the Author - 113

Prologue

You've had a loss in your life. You are trying to learn how to live on your own. You want things the way they were. You're sad, angry, fearful, bitter, all at once. You don't know where you'll find the courage to go it alone.

Grieving feels like you can't catch your breath. Like you are gasping for air.

However long you grieve, you must honor that. At some point, you will want to heal. This book can show you a way.

When you are going through your pain, you are completely stuck in your ache and fear and powerlessness. Every day you try to escape, but you find yourself back in your prison cell each night.

Little by little, moment by moment, day by day, you start to break free. You decide to keep going. At first, you distract yourself to survive. And then, you start making tiny changes, so small no one would notice them. Just you.

Little changes that over time become who you are. And when you start to become who you are, you start to heal. It's a funny thing. When you hang on and stay in pain, and live with a hole in your heart, you cling to what was. You don't heal.

When you start to inch forward, you start to breathe again. Just a little at first. You're reluctant. You don't want to move on. Not alone. And so you stay imprisoned.

But when the day comes that you start living for you, the healing begins. One tiny moment after the next.

We can still hold on to all the memories of the past and honor them as we embark on healing. On finding who we are.

This book understands and is an easy read. There are four sections: Honor Yourself. Believe in Yourself. Be Yourself. Find Yourself.

Each one-page vignette is a moment from my life. This is followed by a Reflection, insights learned from the event, circumstance, or memory.

My healing journey was long. It started when the love of my life left this earth, and I was left with a great big hole in my heart. A great big emptiness in my life. A realization that I was lost. Could I even find myself again? Would I want to?

I was now a "party of one." Forced to go it alone and live my dreams. I think the hardest memories were of those times when my partner and I were doing absolutely nothing together.

I needed to figure out where I had left off, before I was in the best relationship of my life. It was hard work to go back to that. To find the me inside of me.

I got accustomed to life with another person. My perspective was two. And now I had to figure out how to navigate as one.

When we find ourselves alone, we go back to the one thing we have. The thing we've always had. Ourselves.

We start to think about what makes us happy. In time, we begin to daydream about what we want. And we know it's right when it just feels right. When we're content.

Bob, my partner, died in November 2012. Through my healing journey, I learned how to reset, reimagine, and rewrite my life.

My hope is that the words on these pages will help you heal with ease and calm and grace.

And find strength in being a party of one.

Part One

Honor Yourself

You Matter

Be kind and tender

in the caring of you.

Do not forget – You matter.

Honor each moment

of this new journey.

Take time to breathe, to rest,

to begin anew.

Time Is Irrelevant

Learning how to be alone can take a long time. You cannot rush it. And no one can nudge you along.

It took me six years to finally start feeling whole. To feel less empty. Able to move forward without dragging myself through another day.

You must ignore the people that want you to be better quickly so they can have you back.

It's important to honor yourself as you are healing.

Reflection...

If you need time, one day after the next until you are less sad, so be it.

No one can tell you how long this will be. You are like no other. There are no trends to follow. No words. No answers. Just time.

Give yourself permission. Take the time you need.

Being Alone

There is no getting around this. If you have had a deep relationship with someone, you're going to feel their absence when they are gone.

I used to say I enjoyed doing nothing with Bob. I miss even that. The days we did absolutely nothing together.

Embrace that you will feel this absence. Especially on those days you were just together. Doing nothing.

Reflection...

This is a chance to learn the gift of patience.

Patience for yourself.

Wishing You Could Have Done More

No matter what you've done to help your partner, you'll feel there was more you could have done.

The crossword brought Bob great joy. Every day he would tackle it, in pen. He couldn't do this any more. He would carry it around but no words came.

I wanted to help him fill out the crossword. But I couldn't. This was his private time. His own ritual. It left me feeling helpless and empty and sad.

Reflection...

Accept that no matter what we do, it never feels like enough.

Believe that we did all we could.

Allow Friends to Gather

It seemed as if my friends did not leave my side or they turned up just when I needed them.

Let your friends do this for you. They want you to know you're not totally alone even though you have a hole in your heart. They want you to know they love you.

Reflection...

You do not have to carry all of this on your own.

Accept the help, the hugs, the kindness.

When Friends Return to Their Lives

There will be a time when your friends must go back to their lives.

They cannot continue to spend as much time with you.

They got you on your way, and now you must keep moving.

Reflection...

We can continue on without our friends by our side.
We can take one step and then another.

We can start to find our way.

Getting Through the Day

What helped me get through the day was the hope that this would be *the* one where I would feel a little better.

Every day, around 5pm, I would say, "Well, I got through another day." After a year, I said, "Well, I got through a year." And on and on.

Having things to do kept me sane. Distractions were key. Rituals were vital. Morning coffee, going to work, paying bills, grocery shopping. Repeat.

Reflection...

It's good to have something to get out of bed for. Even a good fresh cup of coffee. Sometimes that's enough.

Having a routine will give you structure. That is what you need right now. Make it simple. Just a few things you enjoy every morning to help you start.

Never the Same Again

I wanted to wake up from this ache. Of being alone with the household chores. For so many years, my routine was going to work while Bob took care of, well, everything.

And that was now over. Unskilled and ill-equipped, I had to figure out how I was going to do it all. How I would fill his space.

Reflection...

You don't want it to change. But it does. And you need to find a way. Your way. A new way.

You'll do all of it differently. Maybe better. You have your own unique abilities. Be open. Be kind to yourself.

Wading Through the Bills

Sometimes the amount of bills seemed insurmountable. I did not want to be the one to slog through them. I did not want to make all those calls and send death certificates.

The "business" of it all was overwhelming and made everything a little too real.

Reflection...

Create a way that is less daunting. Try breaking down the larger tasks into smaller ones. One task at a time. And one a day.

And then be pleased with yourself that you did it. You conquered it. Celebrate you.

Fear Keeps Me Here

I was terrified of what was waiting for me on the other side. What is on the other side of grief? I didn't like thinking about that.

I couldn't imagine what life would be like with just me at the helm. I couldn't visualize this. When I looked, I saw darkness. Like the darkness on a stage before the lights come up. Complete and total nothingness.

The uncertainty was enough to make me crawl under the covers. And stay there. And dream about how it was.

Reflection...

We need to be our own cheerleaders. And get ourselves out of bed, and get through one more day.

Because no one is coming to do it for us. No one can. We have to "parent" ourselves and make us do the thing. The task. Live.

It's up to us now.

Special Days

How would I celebrate Bob's birthday, our anniversary, and all the other special dates that we had accumulated over the years?

On these occasions, I would remember funny stories he had told me (I'm smiling now thinking about them), the two of us dancing in the kitchen while waiting for our meat loaf dinner to cook, laughing hysterically at *The Book of Mormon*, and other happy times.

Reflection...

There is a way to embrace and honor and mark these significant dates.

It is different now, but no less special.

Find a way.

Holding Hands

We always held hands.

My small hand fit so perfectly into his long, lean, warm hand.

This was the place we always went back to. And even if we had a disagreement, we always found our way back to each other. Hand in hand.

That was our middle ground. We always found peace there. It brought us back to center.

Reflection...

Remember the intimate moments. The warmth. The love. The oneness.

These thoughts never leave.

They are sacred.

The Creative One

He was the creative one. And when our child, Sydney, had a project from school, Bob was at the ready, with his tools and rulers and pencils. He had wanted to be an architect, and this allowed that creativity to emerge.

As a kid, Bob painted figurines. Napoleon was a favorite. As an adult, he built dollhouses. He was meticulous, and together he and Sydney created spectacular dioramas.

Reflection...

Do your best. You may not measure up, but make every effort to help with projects that need a skill set you may lack.

Do it with joy. And curiosity. And love. And talk about how great your partner was at that sort of thing.

Travel Bound

The years we traveled were magical. Barcelona was his favorite. Paris was mine. We did both and Tuscany too. And Venice, and Cinque Terre, and Antibes, and Monaco... And always with Sydney.

Our trips to New York (where I hailed from) to see theatre were always enormous fun. Our last trip, although we didn't know it at the time, included *Madama Butterfly* at The Met, *The Book of Mormon*, a Hugh Jackman show, and *Seminar*, a play with Alan Rickman, who Sydney managed to snag a picture with.

We packed so much into this trip, as if it were the last. It was.

Reflection...

Treasure the beautiful, magical times together. Recall the amazing adventures you took. Celebrate them. Think of them often. With deep gratitude.

Live your life to the absolute fullest. Squeeze every beautiful drop out. Do not question. Do not wait. Do not put anything off. Just live every day.

A Paradox

Bob had a dry wit, strong beliefs, did not suffer fools, and didn't care if he was liked. (He was liked.)

He was a romantic. He cried each time he watched *Casablanca*, because he loved how Rick fought for the right side and did the right thing (and also loved Ilsa).

He also teared up watching *La Boheme*, his favorite Puccini opera, because the characters were trying to live a free life. (It meant a lot when I decided to walk down the aisle to the beautiful aria "O soave fanciulla.")

I loved his duality.

Reflection...

We can all have a duality of emotions.

We can be tough when we need to be, and cry when that feeling rises up.

We can be courageous and fearful. Confident and sad. Determined and uncertain.

Accept the duality of emotions you may be feeling.

Driving Around

Bob was the main driver and drove the kid everywhere.

He drove Sydney to school, swimming, softball, art, gymnastics, voice, piano, ballet, basketball, acting, and so many other places I'm forgetting.

And then that was gone.

Reflection...

Your heart will hurt because a bond that was once there for your child, and very different than the bond you have, is gone. In an instant you have to fill this huge, gaping hole in your child's heart and life.

Don't try to be your partner. Just be you.

That Voice

The first time I heard Bob's voice was on a phone call. I had just been promoted to the production department of the *New Yorker* magazine. Bob had just transferred to the paper handling department of R.R. Donnelley Chicago, printers for the *New Yorker*.

If it wasn't for a damaged roll of paper, we might never have met at all. He called me to discuss it. And that voice. He had me at hello.

When he was gone, I would listen to his voicemail messages. Over and over again. I loved hearing the lilt in his voice. I missed his deep tones. It was like having him near. It comforted me.

Reflection...

I don't think it's a bad thing, as you're trying to make sense of it all, to listen to their voice. Even if it's just in your head.

It can be quite calming and settling. Do it when you need to. You will stop one day when the time feels right.

Part Two

Believe in Yourself

You Can

You are learning who you are.

Be kind to you. Be generous to you.

Believe in you.

Your true self knows

your strength, your courage,

your resolve.

It knows you can.

Stronger Than You Want to Be

I had become dependent on Bob. Like the feeling you get when you become accustomed to something. Life becomes easy. You don't have to make an effort because you're a team.

I sometimes marveled that I was able to carry on. Get all those medical bills paid. Get the kid through high school. And then find colleges. And continue living.

Every day, I somehow managed to pull myself out of quicksand.

Reflection...

Being strong starts to feel good. Knowing you can do it. Even when you think you can't.

A new pattern starts to slowly emerge. And you are stronger than you thought you could be. Than you wanted to be.

What's for Dinner?

Bob loved the food shopping experience. He knew the grocery clerks by name. With the exception of Thanksgiving, the kitchen was his domain.

Dinner was always a surprise, especially after we'd been on a trip and he was inspired to try a new recipe.

Now I had to take over grocery shopping. I hated grocery shopping. Especially after work. When it was dark. Hated the dark. Had to remember how to cook. And where the hell did he put those recipes?

Reflection...

If you've gotten out of the habit of a task, and the very thought of it makes you queasy, find the best way for you. The easiest way. The simplest way.

You will surprise yourself with your ability to do things you left long ago. You may not find the recipe, but you will create your own.

A Source of Comfort

I had an awful time being surrounded by all the quiet in the house. Loss is loud.

That was very hard. Nerve-wracking. It was so quiet. A different energy. I could not fall asleep. Did not want to close my eyes.

I found that TV was the only way. It was a ready-made community for me. It filled the house with some noise. It comforted me. I left it on all night. For several years.

Reflection...

Do what you need to, to feel okay. To feel less alone. To feel like there are people around you, life around you, filling the silence. Whatever that is for you - TV, music, rain sounds, birds chirping...

No one can tell you how to comfort yourself. You find your way.

Favorites

Bob had favorites.

Some of his were the *New York Times*, including the crossword, which he worked in pen every day. Glenfiddich single malt scotch, unless he was in a Chivas mood, the Cubbies, the Bears, Studs Terkel, *La Boheme*, *Casablanca*, Barcelona, *Victory at Sea*, meat loaf and mashed potatoes, pork tenderloin...

Reflection...

You might keep an eye out for those favorites as a reminder of that beautiful soul.

I remember one time Sydney came down the stairs and saw Bob tearing up. Sydney looked at me and uttered one word: "*Casablanca?*"

Honoring a memory (and smiling) is always a good thing.

Bobisms

"Shit happens" was a good one. Also "people affected by decisions should have input into them," "It's not what happens but how you react that determines your character," "It just be's that way sometimes." "Don't hit the panic button," and "Never complain; never explain."

These were part of his identity. They would pop up now and then, depending on the circumstance. They were grounding. Constant. Like a treasured bookmark or old friend.

Reflection...

It's comforting to write down the "isms" that your loved one said. Or books they quoted from. Or song lyrics they enjoyed.

It's fun to read them once in a while. Especially if they make you laugh. It's good to remember their voice. What made them unique.

Baseball

Baseball was Bob's first love. When he was a kid, he played catcher and was told he didn't have the stuff. What a huge letdown that was.

It was heartening and so fulfilling for him to find TWO baseball teams he could join. One with young guys, and a senior team.

He'd bring Sydney to watch the seniors play, from a seat in the dugout. Sydney would hang out with the players, and one of the wives, a special person to Sydney that, became Grandma Shirley.

Reflection...

I'm so glad he had a chance to play. To do something he loved. To feel euphoric (and like a 10-year-old again) by doing something he was so passionate about.

Everyone deserves this. I'm glad he made it happen in his life, and I cherish this memory.

A New Dining Ritual

I had to create a new dining ritual.

It didn't matter that I wanted the one we had. Eating together, having lovely meals Bob had cooked: crab-stuffed shrimp, beef tenderloin, chicken marengo, crepes filled with asparagus and chicken, mushrooms sautéed with scrambled eggs and served with toast points.

I had to create a new everyday dining ritual. I forced myself to remember my standbys and rotated different meals. Meatballs and spaghetti and breaded chicken became staples.

Reflection...

I can still cook. I can make it easy. I enjoy certain meals and love leftovers. I don't have to make this hard. It won't ever be the same, and I'll always treasure having someone who loved to cook for me. And I miss his food. But I can do this.

And when I'm not in the mood, I treat myself and eat out.

Tears

I couldn't seem to let my tears flow. Of course, I was being strong for Sydney. But there was more. I didn't want to trivialize the moment.

I finally let the tears come at a performance of *Next to Normal* that Sydney and I attended. We'd seen the show before. Knew what to expect. It's achingly sad.

The tears I had been storing for months flowed. I didn't cry. I wailed. Masses of crumpled wet tissues in my hand.

Breaking down broke me open. Gave me a way through from a loss so immense and heavy. Crying in the majesty of a theatre seemed fitting. The right setting for my grief.

Reflection...

Crying. Letting your emotions pour out of you is personal, sacred.

No one can understand why you do or don't cry. No one can judge what you are going through. You have your reasons. Listen to what your heart is telling you. Find your own way through your grief.

No Concentration

I had a hell of a time concentrating. Reading became difficult. Impossible. I was fidgety, anxious. Couldn't sit still. My mind racing. Wondering how I could distract myself. Reading took patience. I needed a quiet activity that didn't need a still mind.

Writing seemed to fill that gap. I could write in a journal. Had plenty of those around. One sentence. One thought. A quote that made me feel better, a song lyric. Anything. Writing made the time pass. It became my distraction ritual that got me through each morning.

Reflection...

Don't be hard on yourself if you're feeling anxious and can't quiet your mind.

You're going through a healing process. Maybe you, too, need something more action oriented while your brain is racing at 90 miles an hour.

Find an activity that can calm you and put you at ease. Make that your ritual. (Ideas: baking, running, gardening, sewing, yoga, walking, drawing.)

Sunday Mornings

Sundays typically started with Will Shortz, the puzzle master. It was part of our ritual, along with coffee. We'd put the radio on and try to guess the answers.

Then the *New York Times*, splayed out on our small dining room table. Bob read it cover to cover. I'd hunt for the Arts & Leisure section. That was my lifeblood.

The coffee made, happily reading the *Times*, the puzzle over, we sometimes put on an opera, maybe *Turandot*, or a little Brubeck. Sydney just added to our joy and a perfect day.

No one thought about work or stress. The biggest quandary was what to make for dinner.

When Bob was gone, those activities seemed out of place, wrong, like wearing two left shoes. Another thing I needed to change. Another memory to miss.

Reflection...

I tried a few times, but it seemed all wrong. The puzzle didn't matter as much without Bob.

I bought the Sunday *New York Times* for a while, but I could not stop seeing him there, in my mind, reading it, pointing out a wonderful editorial. He said the best writing was in the *New York Times*. (For a guy who grew up in Chicago, he was very New York.)

That's when I started to journal. I'd make my coffee, sit in a comfy chair in the living room, and start to write. I might put music on or the TV or listen to a podcast. I missed our Sundays. No getting around that. But in time, I found my way. I found my own peace.

Just Lucky I Guess

Steve Goodman was one of Bob's Chicago heroes. A prolific singer/songwriter, who loved Chicago and wrote several songs about the city, he died way too young.

His song, "Just Lucky I Guess" was one that Bob played for me. It was for us. It was our story.

Every once in a while that song will just pop into my head. I love when that happens. I take that as a sign that Bob's around. And reminding me of those early days in our relationship.

Reflection...

The words in that song make my heart happy. When I look back at how Bob and I met. How coincidental that was. How his life and mine came together at just the perfect time in our lives.

I feel lucky I met Bob. I feel lucky we had Sydney. I feel lucky for the path our life took. And as the song goes...

"How did I let that happen? I was just lucky I guess."

Part Three

Be Yourself

You Shine

*Nothing can dim your light
or diminish you.*

*You are like the stars.
You shine and shine and shine.*

It's Okay to Do Nothing

I found doing nothing to be calming. I needed to. To rest, rejuvenate, recharge. And be ready for the next day.

Reflection...

There is no guilt in doing nothing. You don't need permission from anyone.

You can even set an intention to do nothing for part of your day. Relax, listen to music, or do whatever is not taxing.

Breathe in and out. Slowly. That will serve you.

Party of One

I always loved dining out. Eating in nice restaurants with white tablecloths and a lovely ambience. But when I lost Bob, I had to force myself to eat out. I always took a journal with me to write in. My prop.

At first I was embarrassed to say "just me." In time, I found it empowering to be out as a "party of one."

I was proud to have come this far. To stand on my own. To have gone through this and come out the other side.

Reflection...

Go out in the world and just be who you are. You can stand on your own.

When the maitre d' asks, "How many in your party?" Proudly say, "Party of one!"

Going to the Movies. Alone.

This was a tough one, but when a movie came out that I wanted to see, I just learned to get off the couch and see it. To not wait around to find someone to go with me.

I'd go to an early show. Get some popcorn. Settle into the comfy seat and enjoy the coming attractions.

Reflection...

If going to the movies is hard, think of this as treating yourself. Join the world of make believe and take yourself out on a date.

You deserve it.

Feeling Bad Because You're Feeling Good

I would do something or hear something or read something that made me laugh. That made me have a good time. That made me forget I was sad five minutes ago. This would come in waves.

Reflection...

Stop feeling bad when you feel good. Feeling good, feeling joyful, finding yourself laughing again does not diminish or dishonor your grief.

Do not stop yourself from being happy. This is part of the healing.

Getting Back to Who You Are

I started to do the things I liked doing on my own. Things I never minded doing alone. Things I enjoyed...

Taking walks while listening to music, watching a TV program, journaling, talking with friends, going for coffee, going to the theatre, buying flowers...

Reflection...

You can find things you enjoy doing on your own. You may have to push yourself at first until it becomes a new pattern, but it is worth it.

You are trying to get back to who you are. Just you.
Your true self.

Keeping Memories

Every once in a while, I'll find a piece of paper with Bob's handwriting.

A recipe he jotted down, a letter he wrote me when we were first courting, a Post-it note for Sydney with the word "Hug" written on it (which Sydney later got tattooed on their arm).

He had gorgeous handwriting. I loved looking at it. I keep these little written treasures. They make my heart happy.

Reflection...

Keep the memories you find. Especially when they make you feel good and bring up special times you enjoyed together.

Hold on to them. Celebrate them.

Pardon My French

We were in Normandy, a spot Bob dearly wanted to visit. We stayed at a house where the owners didn't speak any English. Having always prided myself on my French, which meant sentences here and there and a very good try at the accent, I thought I had it licked.

Our hostess gazed at tired little Sydney, and I was sure she offered us dessert, which I happily accepted. When she handed me a carton of eggs, Bob and I looked at each other, both of us realizing my language bungle, and from that point on, any misunderstanding would be met with laughter and, "Dessert?" "No, des oeufs!"

(They can sound similar if you aren't fluent.)

Reflection...

Laughter is restorative and heartening. Even laughing at silly things like "des oeufs," thinking it was a yummy dessert we were being offered.

We'll never have that moment again. We'll never have Normandy again. But eggs will always bring a smile to my face.

Life gives you these little treasures to help you smile and heal. Accept them.

No More Us

I knew who I was a long time ago. Before Bob happened to my life.

Feisty, an independent thinker. I wanted a lot out of life. Had strong values. Knew what I liked. What I didn't.

When I became a partner with the love of my life, I was still feisty and me, but I learned to bend a little more, to listen, to hear Bob's perspective, be open to his desires, likes, dreams.

And then...I found myself without this other person. It's not that he completed me. But he added to what I was. And we blended like a painting. Different colors swirling together to make something beautiful. Not him. Not I. Us.

And all of a sudden that ended. There was no more us.

Reflection...

I found my way back to me slowly. But I had more depth. More color. More vibrancy. Because of Bob.

I was my feisty, fierce, independent self, but there was more dimension, more understanding, more wisdom, more awareness, more fullness.

I found me, but a richer version of me. Because of Bob.

The Chagall Windows

Early in our relationship, on one of my visits to Chicago, Bob introduced me to the Art Institute.

He knew me so well. Knew I would fall in love with the building, with its two bronze lions flanking the grand steps and welcoming visitors, so much like the New York Public Library.

Once inside, he led me to the Chagall windows. The most beautiful wall of stained glass I had ever seen. Awestruck, I sat there for what seemed like weeks, mesmerized by this beauty.

The Art Institute was just one of many Chicago jewels that he would enthusiastically talk about. The aesthetic was all I needed to fall in love with his city.

When I would visit Chicago after he left this earth, I would not miss a chance to check in on my Chagall windows. I would sit there, take in their beauty, and recall when Bob first opened my eyes to this splendor.

Reflection...

All I can say is thank you.

Thank you for sharing your world with me. Thank you for showing me the history and the architecture and the lakefront.

This has enriched my life more than I can say. It has brought me joy. Hope. Dare I say, Nirvana.

There is probably some magic your partner brought to you. Visit it if you can.

The Movie in My Mind

I started to walk him over to the big comfy chair in the bedroom. Just a few feet away from his bed. This had become the morning ritual. Get Bob out of bed. Take tiny shuffling steps until we reached the chair.

You always know when the trajectory of your life changes. When something of such huge proportion drops into your life, unannounced, uninvited, unwelcome.

And like tectonic plates moving under us, he collapsed. His legs stopped working.

The paramedics came and, in one fell swoop, lifted him from the floor back onto his bed.

One of the saddest memories replayed in my mind.

Reflection...

There will be times a memory floods in that is devastatingly sad, painful to relive, and achingly real.

Even in your healing, these moments will rise. Allow them in. Don't push them down.

But try not to let them pull you under their powerful current. Just let them be a moment. Let them come. And then let them float by.

Part Four

Find Yourself

You Soar

You are an amazing being,
becoming more than you
believed possible.

Don't be afraid
to find your true self and
continue to soar.

Sophisticated and Scrappy

He was my date to the theatre, to the opera, to museums. He loved the arts as much as I did. (He also loved baseball, golf, football...)

He was the one who accompanied me to Paris and Barcelona, and all the other amazing places we dreamed about.

Debonair (is that word still used?), loved a tux, stood up when I came into a room, held the door...and showed the most respect to women I have ever witnessed. A staunch believer in women's (and human) rights.

He was my Rick to Ilsa (*Casablanca*), my Bill Sampson to Margo Channing (*All About Eve*). There was something old time about him, sophisticated, urbane, and scrappy. I loved that combination.

I miss it.

Reflection...

I'm a romantic. Always have been. My mom used to say to me when I was a kid, "You love the idea of love." She was right.

And somehow that person I had dreamed about in all those movies came to be. Came into my life. And for the time we had (and it's never enough), I feel blessed, and grateful, and happy that I have lovely memories.

So Many Books

Our dark wood bookshelves resembled the ones in Henry Higgins's library in *My Fair Lady* (another favorite). So many books lived there and would never be read again.

These books were Bob's personal treasures. I kept them for a long time, not wanting to touch them, maybe thinking he'd be back for them.

I needed to let them go.

Reflection...

Giving books away did not diminish their importance. Did not disrespect the words that were so important to Bob. Having the books did not keep him near me, as I was hoping they would.

I finally had to let them find a new home.

Make Your Home Yours

So much of our art we had chosen together. He loved three-dimensional art and art from different cultures. I loved modern art.

It took a lot of strength to remove some of his art from the walls. Took me years. I felt incredibly guilty about it. Like I was betraying him. It was one of the hardest things I tackled.

But in time, I needed to make my home mine.

Reflection...

It's okay to start being you. To let your individual self come out. Decorate your home for you.

Your partner is not going to be upset. Not going to feel betrayed. Not going to wonder where you put their stuff. Your partner is going to smile and say, "It's about time."

Deep in His Heart

I think Sydney is what Bob wanted to be. Fearless, adventurous, daring.

Deep in his heart, he knew. Sydney was the real deal.
All of those things plus talented, artistic, compassionate, original.

Toward the end of his days, he was weak and wasn't able to say very much. But when the hospice director asked him about Sydney, his face changed. He beamed. A grin from ear to ear. And he said "Sydney? That kid is going to be on stage one day, and make it big. You wait and see."

I'll never forget that. I'll never forget those words that he kept deep in his heart.

Reflection...

Even when someone is nearing the end of their days, they know and see everything.

I'm so grateful I was there to hear this. To see Bob smile. To feel what little energy he had pour into this declaration.

And we are both watching the kid soar. Bob from the heavens, and me here on earth.

Letting Go of Stuff

In general, letting go of stuff was quite difficult for me. A large frying pan I'd never use, books, clothing. I found this incredibly hard.

I held on to his tuxedo for so long. As if he was coming back to claim it. And we'd go out once more to a black-tie event.

(I did hold on to his New York subway cuff links and modern-art ties that I had bought for him and have made them my own.)

Reflection...

The longer I held on to his things, the harder it was to become me.

Only hold on to those things you will use, wear, enjoy and make your own.

Scattered Papers

The kitchen counter worked best as Bob's office, even though there was a lovely large desk upstairs. The counter was more convenient. Assorted mail, bills, and the *New York Times*, found a resting place there. Sometimes he'd be looking for something for weeks, only to find it buried under the pile on the counter.

The piles of mail and papers did drive me a little crazy. But it was his sacred spot, so I let it be.

Reflection...

Clean up the papers. You've been wanting to for years. Do it. Find a place for everything. And throw out the junk mail.

You'll either find some buried treasure or a buried bill. Either way, it's okay to take back the kitchen.

Paris on My Own

We traveled several times to Paris. Bob, Sydney, and I. Always loved it. Each time, we found a new restaurant, museum, passage, or park to add to our experience.

We stayed in an apartment in the 7th Arrondissement. It was quaint and had a tiny balcony from which we could see the Eiffel Tower sparkling every night.

The time finally came, five years after his passing, when I had a craving to travel to Paris. Alone. I needed to be back there. I needed to know I could do it. I found the courage. Stayed at the Esmeralda Hotel near Shakespeare and Company in the 5th Arrondissement, diagonal to Notre Dame.

Reflection...

You are able to do big things on your own.

Daunting? Yes. Impulsive? Maybe. And so powerful.

It will lead you to other firsts. And help you be who you are meant to be.

Dear Bob:
Letters of Our Life

I wrote and wrote and wrote. A letter a day for six years. 1,891 letters.

It was my way of talking to him. Holding on to him. Letting him know what was going on. That I paid a bill. That Sydney got into a production of *Rent*, was graduating from high school, got a driver's license, and, was accepted into college. And remembrances of the trips we'd been on, the times he made me laugh, and memories we shared.

Reflection...

You must do what your heart tells you. Mine told me to write to Bob. It soothed me, distracted me, and filled the emptiness.

It was my way of hanging on and letting go.

Celebrate a Life

I always celebrate the anniversary of Bob's passing, dining out at a nice restaurant, usually French, and toasting his memory with a glass of champagne.

I honor him, think about him, celebrate him. This is my special moment to be with him.

Reflection...

Celebrating is your private ceremony.

It's stepping back and seeing your loved one as goodness and humor and warmth and completeness.

Celebrating brings peace and calm and balance. And honors a beautiful life.

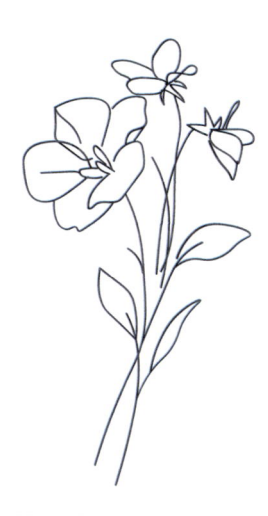

Maybe It's Me

I had been journaling quite a lot and thinking about a move to Chicago. I was wondering why I was feeling a need to be back there. Of course, I loved it. Loved the lakefront. Loved the architecture. Loved the vibrancy of the city.

But, what was pulling me? What could the reason be? I even wrote, "Maybe it's to find someone."

And then, my pen kept writing...
"Maybe it's me."

Reflection...

I somehow knew (or my pen did) the reason to move back to Chicago was to find *me* again. The me I had left there years ago.

Your heart will always know the way, the path, the reason. Follow it. Always.

The Big Move

I decided to go back to where we began. I always knew I would.

So in my 10th year without Bob, I moved back to Chicago. Where he was from. Where we had several blissful years. And I'm living here on my own. As a "party of one."

Reflection...

Don't rush your healing. Be patient with yourself.
Love yourself. Be kind to yourself.

And when it's time, move on. Emotionally, mentally, physically.

You will be ready.

Epilogue

It took me six years to heal, meaning, to find my way.
In that time, the letters I wrote helped me get through each day. Hard to believe I wrote in 43 journals, 1,891 letters.

During this healing time, Sydney got a driver's license, was in several theatre productions, graduated from high school, and decided on Loyola Chicago for college after we had gone for a weekend to see one of their theatre productions.

Sydney is a graphic designer and composer/performer, under the name Bigkid. Sydney's first EP is called "Anecdotal."

I was having strong feelings about becoming a coach, to put to use leadership skills from my work experience and the new mindset I had developed from my healing journey.

I started to fix up my townhouse in Kirkland, WA, knowing that, at some point, I would be headed back to the only place I really belonged - Chicago.

I finally made my move back, 10 years after Bob's death, in July 2022, oddly enough the same weekend I first came to Chicago from New York, back in 1985 - the July 4th weekend.

I am happily settling back into Chicago, feeling grateful every day for my beautiful life.

I always used to say about Kirkland, that I just stayed at the party too long. We were a great team, he and I. But I needed to find my place, somewhere that aligned with who I was.

On one of my first trips to Chicago, when Bob and I had just met and he wanted to impress me with his city, he introduced me to the Art Institute and the stunning Chagall windows.

I don't know if that's what hooked me or if it was the gorgeous architecture overlooking the lake, or saganaki (flaming cheese) in Greektown, but I fell in love with his city.

Now back in Chicago, when I take walks and pass by the opera house or by buildings or restaurants and theatre, that we used to enjoy together, I feel filled with possibility. I can breathe. I'm at ease.

Sometimes I'll say, "Bob, what is that building over there?" Or, "Remember when you took me here for my birthday?" The memories flood back. They're beautiful and make my heart happy.

I am glad to be back and thriving as a "party of one."

Loss Is Loud

The loss was so loud. Deafening.

Talking to myself. Or to the TV.
Distraction was my best friend.

One step and then another.
Finding my way. Alone.

Not wanting to be strong.
Not wanting to rely on me.

But time passes. And magic happens.

And one day
I start to make things my own.

Being proud of my choices.
Stepping up. Showing up. As my true self.

And then a leap to Paris. On my own.
And it was good.

And a leap to move.
To move back to where it began.

To sweet home Chicago. Where Bob was from.
Where we lived in bliss. A long time ago.

And I can pick up where I left off. Sort of.
And fill my heart with joy. And know who I am.

And show up as me. The me now. And I feel good.

As a party of one.

-Sheila Kamuda

Acknowledgements

Thanks to Carrie Urbanic for being another set of eyes on a work that is so dear to my heart. I have great appreciation for her editing skill, thoughtful suggestions, and her care in honoring my voice throughout the editing process.

About the Author

Sheila Kamuda is an empowerment coach, founder of Live Out Loud Coaching, speaker, and author of *My Badass Journal*, *My Badass Gratitude Journal*, and *The Little Book of Badass Feelings*.

Originally from New York, and a theatre junkie through and through, Sheila's healing journey brought her back to where it all began, and she now lives in "sweet home Chicago."

Sheila felt this book wanted to be written for those who have had a loss, are struggling to find a way through, and trying to learn how to be on their own.

She hopes her words meet you where you are, and are a guide through your healing journey.

Made in United States
Troutdale, OR
02/23/2025